First Steps To Understanding

Nahw

Hashim Muhammad

Al-Qalam Publications

First Steps To Understanding Nahw
First Edition April, 2016

Video lectures for this book is available on our YouTube Channel www.youtube.com/c/AlQalamInstitute

ISBN: 978-0-9576534-6-7

Compiler	**Hashim Muhammad**
Contact:	**Al-Qalam Institute**
	28 Melbourne Road,
	Leicester, LE2 0DR,
	United Kingdom

Email	info@alqalaminstitute.org
Website	http://alqalaminstitute.org
Mobile/Whatsapp	+44 7507859443

If you see any mistakes in this book, have any comments or suggestions, please feel free to contact us. Jazakallah.

Printed by Mega Printing in Turkey

Contents

3

بِسْمِ اللّٰهِ الرَّحْمٰنِ الرَّحِيْمِ

Reason for Writing This Book

Many books on the subject of Nahw have been written in English. However, to the best of my knowledge, most of them are based on classical Arabic texts on Nahw or translations of these texts. However, I felt there was a need for a book to be written specifically for English speakers.

I have laid out the contents of this book, to the best of my ability, in a manner which will, insha'allah, appeal to an English speaker and relate in some way to English grammar.

Note for Teachers

This book is meant to be an introduction to Nahw. It is not a comprehensive text book which covers all the technical issues of the language. Hence, we have tried to simplify this book as much as possible. We have omitted many things and in many cases we have simplified the rules to a very basic level. We humbly request you not to overburden the student with additional information. This would completely negate the point of this book.

Similarly, we **beseech** the teachers not to make students memorise this book word for word. It is not a holy script that needs to be preserved; Nahw is a science which needs to be understood!

Note for Students

As mentioned above, this is an entry level book. You will need to study other texts to fully understand the language properly. The objective of this book is to give you a brief overview of how the Arabic language works. Secondly, the rules in this book are all simplified rules to which you will find more details and exceptions as you study Nahw in more detail.

SECTION 1
Types Of Words

Arabic Words

In Arabic a word is called كَلِمَةٌ. The plural is كَلِمَاتٌ. Words are divided into three categories: nouns, verbs and particles.

1) Noun: a thing e.g. pen, paper.

   A noun is called an اِسْمٌ. The plural is أَسْمَاءٌ.

   Nouns will have either an ال at the beginning or a تنوين at the end.

رَسُوْلٌ   اَلرَّسُوْلُ

2) Verb: an action. e.g. run, sat.

   A verb is called a فِعْلٌ. The plural is أَفْعَالٌ.

   Verbs will come on one of the following patterns:

اِفْتَحْ   يَفْتَحُ   فَتَحَ

3) Particle: usually a two letter word which is added to nouns and verbs. e.g. إِلَى, فِيْ.

   A particle is called a حَرْفٌ. The plural is حُرُوْفٌ.

Arabic Words		كَلِمَاتٌ		
Nouns اِسْمٌ		Verb فِعْلٌ		Particle حَرْفٌ
Name, Thing		Action		Two Letter Words
ال	تنوين	فَتَحَ يَفْتَحُ اِفْتَحْ		فِيْ، إِلَى

Nouns

Nouns can be studied from different perspectives. Here, we are going to look at four important characteristics of nouns: 1) Definite – Indefinite 2) Gender 3) Number 4) I'raab.

Characteristic 1
Definite and Indefinite

1) Definite: a name or a thing with **the** before it.

Muhammad   *the pen*

In Arabic, the اَلْ at the beginning of a noun is equal to the English word **the**.

اَلنَّبِيُّ   اَلرَّسُوْلُ

the prophet   *the messenger*

A definite noun is called مَعْرِفَة.

2) Indefinite: a noun with the letter **a** before it.

a pen

In Arabic, the تنوين at the end of a word is equal to the English word **a**.

نَبِيٌّ   رَسُوْلٌ

a prophet   *a messenger*

An indefinite noun is called نَكِرَة.

Look at the following verse and see how a noun has been used first as نكرة then معرفة.

﴿أَرْسَلْنَا إِلَى فِرْعَوْنَ رَسُوْلًا فَعَصَى فِرْعَوْنُ الرَّسُوْلَ﴾

*We sent **a** messenger to Fir'awn. Then, Fir'awn disobeyed **the** messenger.*

Characteristic 2
Gender

All living things have a natural gender i.e. they will be either masculine or feminine.

Masculine	Feminine
وَلَدٌ	بِنْتٌ
boy	girl

In Arabic, non-living things also have a grammatical gender i.e. even though they are neither male nor female, for grammatical purposes they are considered as eithier masculine or feminine.

Feminine Nouns

Nouns will be considered feminine in the following cases:

1. By natural gender i.e. if it refers to a female person.

أُمٌّ   مَرْيَمُ

mother   Maryam

2. If it has a round ة at the end:

أُمَّةٌ

a nation

The Arabic term for feminine is مُؤَنَّث.

Masculine Nouns

Apart from these two types of nouns, all other nouns are masculine. The Arabic name for masculine is مُذَكَّر.

Characteristic 3
Singular, Dual and Plural

A noun can be singular, dual or plural. You already know what singular and plurals are, as these terms are also used in English.

Singular

Singular nouns are called وَاحِدٌ.

Duals

In Arabic, there is another form of noun that shows two. This is known as dual. Duals are made from the وَاحِد by placing a فَتْحَة on the last letter of the word and then adding انِ.

رَجُلَانِ	⇦	رَجُلٌ
two men		man

A dual word will never have a تنوين. It can however have a ال. Therefore, if it has ال it will be معرفة and if it does not have ال it will be نكرة, even though it does not have a تنوين.

نكرة	معرفة
رَجُلَانِ	الرَّجُلَانِ
two me	*the two men*

If انِ is added to a word ending with a round ة, it will be written like a normal ت.

جَنَّتَانِ	⇦	جَنَّةٌ
two heavens		*heaven*

A dual is called تَثْنِيَةٌ.

Plurals

There are two types of plurals in Arabic; regular and irregular.

1) A regular plural is one that follows a fixed pattern. This type is called اَلْجَمْعُ السَّالِمُ. This is used for both مذكر and مؤنث words.

The masculine version, اَلْجَمْعُ الْمُذَكَّرُ السَّالِمُ, is made by placing a ضمة on the last letter of the واحد; and then by adding وْنَ.

مُسْلِمُوْنَ ⇐ مُسْلِمٌ

believers   *a believer*

The feminine version, اَلْجَمْعُ الْمُؤَنَّثُ السَّالِمُ, is made by removing the ة, placing a فتحة on the last letter, and then by adding اتٌ.

مُؤْمِنَاتٌ ⇐ مُؤْمِنَةٌ

Remember, the round ة / ﺔ is a sign of a singular word being مؤنث; and the اﺕ is a sign of a plural word being مؤنث.

مُسْلِمَاتٌ ⇐ مُسْلِمَةٌ

believing women   a believing woman

2) An irregular plural is one that is formed irregularly, i.e. it has no fixed pattern. This is called اَلْجَمْعُ الْمُكَسَّرُ.

رُسُلٌ ⇐ رَسُوْلٌ   أَنْهَازٌ ⇐ نَهْرٌ

There is no rule to these plurals; they have to be learnt.

Summary of Number of Nouns

جمع **Plural**			تثنية **Dual**		واحد **Singular**	
مكسر	سالم					
	مؤنث	مذكر	مؤنث	مذكر	مؤنث	مذكر
رُسُلٌ	(مُسْلِمَاتٌ)	(مُسْلِمُوْنَ)	(مُسْلِمَتَانِ)	(مُسْلِمَانِ)	(مُسْلِمَةٌ)	(مُسْلِمٌ)

Characteristic 4
I'rab

In Arabic, words end with a vowel i.e. فتحة, ضمة or كسرة due to different rules you will study later.

If a word ends with ضَمَّة, ـٌ, it is generally مَرْفُوْعٌ.

الرَّسُوْلُ   رَسُوْلٌ

If a word ends with فَتْحَة, ـً, it is generally مَنْصُوْبٌ.

الرَّسُوْلَ   رَسُوْلًا

If a word ends with كَسْرَة, ـٍ, it is generally مَجْرُوْرٌ.

الرَّسُوْلِ   رَسُوْلٍ

These three, مرفوع, منصوب and مجرور, are grammatical states. In Arabic this is called إِعْرَابٌ.

Key Words

Definite / Indefinite		Gender		Number		إعراب
Definite	معرفة	Masculine	مذكر	Singular	واحد	مرفوع
Indefinite	نكرة	Feminine	مؤنث	Dual	تثنية	منصوب
				Plural	جمع	مجرور
				Regular	سالم	

Irregular	مكسر

Verbs

A verb, فعل, is a word that shows an action:

hit, run, sleep, etc.

In Arabic, there are three types of verbs:

1. اَلْمَاضِيْ: the past tense. This shows that an action took place in the past.

فَتَحَ

He opened.

2. اَلْمُضَارِعُ: present or future tense.

يَفْتَحُ

He opens, he will open.

3. اَلْأَمْرُ: instruction or command.

اِفْتَحْ

Open!

The rules of each of these will be discussed in صرف in more detail.

Particles

حُرُوْفٌ are particles which join nouns and verbs to give additional meaning to them. Different particles will be discussed when necessary throughout this book.

SECTION 2
Sentences

Until now we have been studying single words. Now, we are going to put different types of words together and make sentences. In Arabic, a sentence is called a جُمْلَةٌ.

There are two types of sentences.

1) اَلْجُمْلَةُ الْإِسْمِيَّةُ: This is a sentence that begins with an اسم.
2) اَلْجُمْلَةُ الْفِعْلِيَّةُ: This is a sentence that begins with a فعل.

الجملة الإسمية

الجملة الإسمية is a sentence which is made up of two parts, the مُبْتَدَأٌ and the خَبَرٌ.

The مبتدأ is the **subject** i.e. the thing you are talking about.

The خبر is the information regarding the مبتدأ.

[The Prophet]مبتدأ is [truthful]خبر

The following rules apply regarding مبتدأ-خبر:

1) The مبتدأ is generally معرفة,
2) The خبر is generally نكرة,
3) The خبر agrees with the مبتدأ in number and gender,
4) Both words are مرفوع.

فَاطِمَةُ صَادِقَةٌ	الرَّسُولُ صَادِقٌ	مُحَمَّدٌ رَسُولٌ
Fatima is truthful.	The Prophet is truthful.	Muhammad ﷺ is a Prophet.

التركيب

The word تركيب literally means to build or to put together. In Nahw, we do تركيب of sentences i.e. we do a grammatical breakdown of the structure of a sentence. Below is the تركيب of a جملة إسمية.

[[مُحَمَّدٌ]مبتدأ [رَسُولٌ]خبر] جملة إسمية

You would express the تركيب in the following way:

محمد is the مبتدأ; رسول is the خبر; and the مبتدأ and خبر join to become a جُمْلَةٌ إِسْمِيَّةٌ.

الجملة الفعلية

الجملة الفعلية is a sentence which starts with a verb. A جملة فعلية has four parts; verb, subject, object and adverb.

Subject

Every فعل must have a subject, someone who is carrying out the action. In Arabic, the subject in الجملة الفعلية is called فَاعِلٌ.

The فاعل comes after the verb and it is مرفوع.

[[قَتَلَ]فعل [دَاؤُوْدُ]فاعل]جملة فعلية

Dawud ﷺ *killed.*

Object

Some verbs may also carry an object, someone upon whom the action is carried out. This is called مَفْعُوْلٌ. The مفعول will be منصوب, and it generally comes after the فاعل.

[[قَتَلَ]فعل [دَاؤُوْدُ]فاعل [جَالوتَ]مفعول]جملة فعلية

(the Prophet) Dawud ﷺ *killed Goliath.*

Note:

In الجملة الإسمية the subject is called مبتدأ, and in الجملة الفعلية the subject is called فاعل. In English they are both called **subject**.

Adverb

Along with a مفعول a جملة فعلية can also have an adverb i.e. something to show time or place. This is called ظَرْفٌ.

﴿لَبِثْنَا يَوْمًا﴾

We have stayed a day.

Recap

We have now covered six main parts of sentences:

1. مبتدأ: This is always a noun and is always مرفوع.

2. خبر: This is always a noun and is always مرفوع.

3. فعل: The rules of this will be discussed in *Sarf*.

4. فاعل: This is always a noun and is always مرفوع.

5. مفعول: This is always a noun and is always منصوب.

6. ظرف: This is always a noun and is always منصوب.

	خبر (مرفوع)	مبتدأ (مرفوع)	جملة إسمية
ظرف (منصوب)	مفعول (منصوب)	فاعل (مرفوع)	فعل	جملة فعلية

SECTION 3
Phrases

Phrases

You would have noticed that five of the six main parts of a sentence are nouns. However, just as they can be single nouns they can also be phrases. Look at the following example:

[The boy]مبتدأ is [clever]خبر.

[This boy]مبتدأ is [a clever student]خبر.

In the first sentence we have two nouns, the first is مبتدأ and the second is خبر. In the second sentence both the مبتدأ and the خبر are made up of two words. These are called **phrases**. These phrases are made up of different nouns and different forms of nouns. The phrase then takes the place of one of the main parts of the sentence i.e. in a جملة فعلية a phrase can take the place of فاعل, مفعول or ظرف, and in جملة إسمية it can take the place of the مبتدأ or خبر.

There are five types of phrases:

1. Descriptive.
2. Demonstrative Phrase.
3. Possessive Phrase.
4. Conjunction.
5. شِبْهُ جُمْلَةٍ.

Descriptive Phrase

The descriptive phrase is made by bringing an adjective i.e. describing word after the noun. In Arabic a describing word is called a صِفَة and it comes after the word it is describing, the مَوْصُوفٌ. The صفة matches the موصوف

in all four characteristic mentioned in section one i.e.

مرفوع-منصوب-مجرور and واحد-تثنية-جمع, مذكر-مؤنث, معرفة-نكرة.

[أَمَةٌ]موصوف [مُؤْمِنَةٌ]صفة

[عَبْدٌ]موصوف [مُؤْمِنٌ]صفة

a believing servant

a believing servant

As mentioned before, a موصوف-صفة can be used wherever a single noun can be used.

اللهُ [إِلٰهٌ وَاحِدٌ]خبر

[اَلْعَبْدُ الْمُؤْمِنُ]مبتدا خَيْرٌ

Allah is a [single deity].

[The believing slave] is better.

قَرَأَ خَالِدٌ [الْقُرْآنَ الْكَرِيْمَ]مفعول

قَالَ [رَجُلٌ مُؤْمِنٌ]فاعل

Khalid read the noble Quran.

The believing man said

Demonstrative Phrase

The demonstrative phrase is made by adding a pointing word, إِسْمُ الْإِشَارَةِ, before the noun.

This is very similar to an adjective in the way it describes the noun.

this man   *smart man*

However there are a few differences:

1. There are innumerable adjectives. However there are only twelve اسم الإشارة. There are six for pointing to close things, these are called اَلْقَرِيْب; and there are six for pointing to far things, these are called اَلْبَعِيْد.

المُؤَنَّثُ			المُذَكَّرُ			⇐
جمع	تثنية	واحد	جمع	تثنية	واحد	
هٰؤُلَاءِ	هَاتَانِ	هٰذِهِ	هٰؤُلَاءِ	هٰذَانِ	هٰذَا	**اَلْقَرِيبُ** This /These
These	This	These	This			
أُولٰئِكَ	تَانِكَ	تِلْكَ	أُولٰئِكَ	ذَانِكَ	ذٰلِكَ	**اَلْبَعِيدُ** That /Those
Those	That	Those	That			

2. In موصوف-صفة the noun comes first and the adjective second; however, in اسم الإشارة-مشار إليه the noun comes after the اسم الإشارة.

[هٰذا]اسم الإشارة [القُرْآنُ]مشار إليه

this Qur'an

3. The اسم الإشارة is معرفة (without the need for an ال) so the word after it, مُشار إليه, must always have the definite article (ال).

4. The اسم الإشارة are fixed words. i.e. they don't take فتحة-ضمة-كسرة, they remain the same in all cases. Any word that behaves like this is called مَبْنِيٌّ.

Here are some examples of اسم الإشارة-مشار إليه being used in different places in the sentence.

أَنْزَلْنَا [هَذَا الْقُرْآنَ]مفعول

We revealed this Qur'an.

[هٰذَا النَّبِيُّ]مبتدا صَادِقٌ

This Prophet is truthful.

The possessive phrase, اَلْإِضَافَةُ, is made by placing the owner after the item that is owned.

[بَيْتُ]المضاف [اللهِ]المضاف إليه

The house of Allah

The first word is called مُضَافٌ, and the second word is called مُضَافٌ إِلَيْهِ.

اَلْمُضَافُ will never have an ال nor a تنوين. The المضاف إليه will be مجرور.

Here are some examples of مضاف-مضاف إليه being used in different places in the sentence.

تَقْتُلُونَ [أَنْبِيَاءَ اللَّهِ]مفعول   مُحَمَّدٌ [رَسُولُ اللَّهِ]خبر

You are killing the Prophets of Allah.   *Muhammad ﷺ is the Messenger of Allah.*

Conjunction

The particle وَ (and) can be used to join two words or phrases together to make a single phrase. This is called عَطْفٌ. The وَ is called حَرْفُ الْعَطْفِ.

[مُحَمَّدٌ وَنُوحٌ]مبتدأ نَبِيَّانِ

Muhammad ﷺ and Nooh ﷺ are two prophets.

The first word is called مَعْطُوفٌ عَلَيْهِ and the second is called مَعْطُوْفٌ.

[[مُحَمَّدٌ]معطوف عليه [وَ]حرف العطف [نُوحٌ]معطوف]مبتدأ نَبِيَّانِ

Another type of phrase is called شِبْهُ الْجُمْلَة. Unlike the other phrases, this is not made up of two nouns, rather it consists of a particle and a noun. These particles are called اَلْحُرُوْفُ الْجَارَّةِ. The word after الحروف الجارة is مَجْرُوْرٌ.

These particles are:

فِيْ: in

فِيْ هٰذَا الْقُرْآنِ

in this Qur'an

عَلَى: on

عَلَىٰ سُرُرٍ

on couches

إِلَى: to, until

إِلَى حِينٍ

until a time

مِنْ: from

مِنْ نَارٍ

from fire

بِ: with

بِسْمِ اللهِ

with the name of Allah.

حَتَّى: until, till

حَتَّىٰ مَطْلَعِ الْفَجْرِ

till the debut of dawn

لِ: for, belongs to

لِرَسُولٍ

for a messenger

عَنْ: regarding, from

عَنِ الْخَمْرِ

regarding alcohol

The تركيب of a شبه الجملة is as follows:

[[فِيْ] حرف جار [الْأَرْضِ] مجرور] شبه جملة

Even though the شبه الجملة is a phrase it cannot replace any noun, unlike the other phrases. Rather it is limited to two places in a sentence:

1) The خبر in الجملة الإسمية.

[الْحَمْدُ] مبتدأ [لِلَّهِ] خبر

Praise is for Allah.

2) The adverb of a فعل in الجملة الفعلية. In this case the شبه الجملة is called a مُتَعَلِّقٌ.

أَرْسَلْنَا نُوحًا [إِلَى الْقَوْمِ] متعلق

We sent Nuh ﷺ to the nation.

Now we have learnt five parts of a جملة فعلية.

متعلق	ظرف	مفعول	فاعل		جملة فعلية
(شبه الجملة)	(منصوب)	(منصوب)	(مرفوع)	فعل	

24

SECTION 4
Pronouns

Just as a phrase can take the place of a noun, a pronoun can also take the place of a noun. A pronoun, ضَمِيْرٌ, is a word which takes the place of a noun.

Pronouns As مبتدأ	*Pronoun As* مفعول	*Pronoun As* مضاف إليه
Zaid is clever.	Ahmad saw Yunus.	Bilal's book
He is clever.	Ahmad saw him.	His book

There are three sets of fourteen pronouns.

اَلضَّمِيْرُ الْمَرْفُوْعُ		اَلضَّمِيْرُ الْمَنْصُوْبُ		اَلضَّمِيْرُ الْمَجْرُوْرُ	
هُوَ	He	هُ	Him	هِ	His
هُمَا	They	هُمَا	Them	هُمَا	Their
هُمْ	They	هُمْ	Them	هُمْ	Their
هِيَ	She	هَا	Her	هَا	Hers
هُمَا	They	هُمَا	Them	هُمَا	Their
هُنَّ	They	هُنَّ	Them	هُنَّ	Their
أَنْتَ	You	كَ	You	كَ	Your
أَنْتُمَا	You	كُمَا	You	كُمَا	Your
أَنْتُمْ	You	كُمْ	You	كُمْ	Your
أَنْتِ	You	كِ	You	كِ	Your
أَنْتُمَا	You	كُمَا	You	كُمَا	Your
أَنْتُنَّ	You	كُنَّ	You	كُنَّ	Your
أَنَا	I	نِيْ / يْ	Me	يْ	My
نَحْنُ	We	نَا	Us	نَا	Our

Pronouns are مبني i.e. the end of the word doesn't change from ضمة to فتحة etc. Instead, there are three different sets of pronouns, one for مرفوع, one for منصوب and one for مجرور.

الضمير المرفوع

The مرفوع pronoun will be used in place of a مبتدأ.

[أَنْتَ]مبتدأ عَلَّامُ الْغُيُوبِ

You (Allah) are the knower of the unseen.

الضمير المنصوب

The منصوب pronoun is used in place of a مفعول. However, it is not used on its own like the مرفوع pronoun. Instead it comes joined to the فعل. In this case, the sentence order changes to فعل–مفعول–فاعل.

خَلَقَكَ اللهُ

Allah created you.

الضمير المجرور

A مجرور pronoun can be used either as the مضاف إليه or the مجرور after حرف جار. Like the منصوب pronoun, it will not come on its own; rather it must be joined to the حرف جار or مضاف.

إِلَيْكَ

towards you

فِي رَحْمَتِكَ

In your mercy

SECTION 5
Sentences within Sentences

Just as a phrase can take the place of a noun, it is also possible for a sentence to take the place of one of the five slots of a noun i.e. a sentence can become a مبتدأ, خبر, فاعل, مفعول or ظرف.

A Sentence as a خبر

A جملة فعلية can become the خبر of a مبتدأ.

[[اللهُ]مبتدأ [رَفَعَ السَّمَاءَ]جملة فعلية/خبر]جملة إسمية

Allah raised the heavens.

The translation of such sentences will be like a normal جملة فعلية and not a جملة اسمية i.e. it won't have is or are.

Note:

A خبر normally ends in a ضمة. However, when the خبر is a sentence it won't have a ضمة.

A Sentence as a مفعول

If the verb of a sentence is the word قَالَ or يَقُوْلُ (to say) then the entire quotation becomes the مفعول.

قَالَ الرَّجُلُ [خَلَقَ اللهُ السَّمَاءَ]مفعول/جملة فعلية   قَالَ الرَّجُلُ [اللهُ رَبٌّ]مفعول/جملة إسمية

A Sentence as مضاف إليه

A مضاف إليه can also come in the form of a sentence:

[يَوْمَ]مضاف [[يَجْمَعُ]فعل [اللهُ]فاعل [الرُّسُلَ]مفعول]مضاف إليه

The day Allah will gather the prophets...

الاسم الموصول

A sentence can also take the position of a noun when an اِسْمُ الْمَوْصُوْل comes before it.

The الأسماء الموصولة are as follows:

مؤنث			مذكر		
جمع	تثنية	واحد	جمع	تثنية	واحد
اللَّاتِيْ	اللَّتَانِ	الَّتِيْ	الَّذِيْنَ	اللَّذَانِ	الَّذِيْ

Think of الاسم الموصول as the ال of sentences i.e. it makes it معرفة.
الاسم الموصول changes to agree with the word that is being spoken about.

The sentence which comes after the اسم الموصول is called the صِلَةٌ. The موصول–صلة then become a صفة.

نَصَرْتُ [الرَّجُلَ] موصوف [[الَّذِيْ] اسم الموصول [جَاءَ مِنَ الْمَدِيْنَةِ] صلة] صفة

I helped the man who came from Madeenah.

SECTION 6
Joining Sentences Together

Until now, we have studied sentences on their own. These were الجملة الفعلية or الجملة الإسمية. Now we are going to discuss how to join sentences together.

Conjunctions

Just as a حرف العطف is used to join two words together to make a phrase, it is also used to join two complete sentences together.

The main particle of عطف is وَ, (and)

[مَا قَتَلُوهُ] وَ[مَا صَلَبُوهُ]

They did not kill him, and they did not crucify him.